Vampires

New and future titles in the series include:

Alien Abductions

Angels

The Bermuda Triangle

The Curse of King Tut

ESP

Haunted Houses

King Arthur

UFOs

Unicorns

Witches

The Mystery Library

Vampires

Russell Roberts

Lucent Books, Inc.
P.O. Box 289011, San Diego, California

On cover: Edvard Munch: *Vampire* 1893–94
Oil on canvas 91 x 109 cm
Munch Museum, Oslo

Library of Congress Cataloging-in-Publication Data

Roberts, Russell, 1953–
    Vampires / by Russell Roberts.
        p. cm. — (The mystery library)
Includes bibliographical references and index.
    Summary: Discusses the origins of the vampire, the vampire
experience, vampires in pop culture, and whether vampires can
be explained.
    ISBN 1-56006-835-3 (hardback : alk. paper)
    1. Vampires. [1. Vampires.] I. Title. II. Mystery library
(Lucent Books)
    GR830.V3 R63 2001
    398 '.45—dc21   00-11963

Contents

Foreword

In Shakespeare's immortal play, *Hamlet*, the young Danish aristocrat Horatio has clearly been astonished and disconcerted by his encounter with a ghost-like apparition on the castle battlements. "There are more things in heaven and earth," his friend Hamlet assures him, "than are dreamt of in your philosophy."

Many people today would readily agree with Hamlet that the world and the vast universe surrounding it are teeming with wonders and oddities that remain largely outside the realm of present human knowledge or understanding. How did the universe begin? What caused the dinosaurs to become extinct? Was the lost continent of Atlantis a real place or merely legendary? Does a monstrous creature lurk beneath the surface of Scotland's Loch Ness? These are only a few of the intriguing questions that remain unanswered, despite the many great strides made by science in recent centuries.

Lucent Books' Mystery Library series is dedicated to exploring these and other perplexing, sometimes bizarre, and often disturbing or frightening wonders. Each volume in the series presents the best-known tales, incidents, and evidence surrounding the topic in question. Also included are the opinions and theories of scientists and other experts who have attempted to unravel and solve the ongoing mystery. And supplementing this information is a fulsome list of sources for further reading, providing the reader with the means to pursue the topic further.

The Mystery Library will satisfy every young reader's fascination for the unexplained. As one of history's greatest scientists, physicist Albert Einstein, put it:

> The most beautiful thing we can experience is the mysterious. It is the source of all true art and science. He to whom this emotion is a stranger, who can no longer wonder and stand rapt in awe, is as good as dead: his eyes are closed.

The Enduring Power of the Vampire

Belief in vampires is almost as old as humanity itself. While vampires are traditionally thought of as reanimated corpses that return to life and drink the blood of the living for sustenance, this definition only refers to the European idea of a vampire and not those from other cultures. Stories about the dead returning to prey upon the living, as well as the power of blood to sustain life, can be found in the most ancient cultures. As civilization developed, the belief in vampires developed with it. Even the word "vampire" has its roots in numerous cultures, such as Hungarian (*vampyr*), Russian (*upyr*), Dutch (*vampir*), and Polish (*wampir*). The vampire itself, however, appears in tales and legends from the Far East to Europe and Scandinavia.

As the concept of the vampire spread, its image gradually became standardized as a corpse rising from the grave. But no matter what culture gave rise to the vampire stories, the creature's intent was the same: to bring harm, illness, and even death to the living.

Even during the twentieth century, when science and rational thought made enormous strides throughout the

world, vampires have remained active in people's imaginations even as other mythical creatures, such as unicorns and fairies, faded into the mist of disbelief. In 1931 the opening of the film *Dracula*, starring Bela Lugosi, was such a great success that it saved its maker, Universal Studios, from bankruptcy. Many in the audiences for this film were members of a generation that had witnessed some of the greatest technological advances in history, such as the invention of the airplane and the automobile, but they still flocked to—and were scared by—a film about a creature that science had long since dismissed.

While there are few organizations dedicated to other mythical creatures, vampire societies, groups, and clubs continue to flourish. What is it about vampires that enables these creatures to remain popular today and maintain their mysterious hold on humanity?

Perhaps the key to the vampire's continuing appeal is the ancient fear of the dead returning to life. Or, conversely, maybe it's the vampire's triumph over death that keeps people enthralled; after all, humankind has been trying to cheat death since the beginning of time.

The fact that belief and interest in vampires have survived from the dawn of human existence to today's computer age illustrates the enormous influence that the vampire has on the human psyche. At its most basic form, the idea of vampires is one of the most enduring of all human concepts—and one of its most primal fears.

Chapter 1

The Vampire Experience

The image of a vampire as a corpse that rises from the grave at night to feast on human blood has become ingrained in the minds of most people in the West today. However, vampires as they are envisioned by many cultures vary widely. Even with these differences, it is still possible to find similarities between the various types of vampires. Whatever their differences and similarities, these mythical creatures reflect some of the most deeply held fears of human beings.

Lust for Blood

Undoubtedly, the most widely held belief is that vampires have an insatiable lust for human blood. Many cultures have stories of such creatures. For instance, Malaysians believed in the *polong*, a female creature just one inch tall. In exchange for a daily supply of blood sucked from a person's finger, the *polong* would perform various tasks, including attacking the person's enemies. (Usually the *polong* worked in conjunction with the cricketlike *pelesit*. The *pelesit* would invade the body of a person about to be attacked by the *polong* and prepare the way for its accomplice.)

Another region with tales of bloodsucking vampires is Africa, where illness was sometimes thought to be caused by an attack from vampire witches. These creatures were

Most Western cultures are familiar with the idea of vampires rising from graves or from crypts, such as this one in England.

supposedly able to leave their human bodies and send their spirits forth in search of victims. When they found one, they would enter the unfortunate's house through the roof and then slip into the victim's body through the stomach. Once inside they would wound the vital organs with spears and also suck the person's blood. The victim would sicken and ultimately die.

In some cultures the vampire's blood lust is thought to explain a lack of energy in a person. In India, for example, the vampire entity known as a *chedipe* was believed to enter the home of a sleeping man and suck the blood out of his toe. The man would awaken feeling tired and disoriented, almost as if intoxicated. If he did not find treatment for this condition, the *chedipe* would return.

Sometimes, inflicting itself on one person at a time is not enough to satisfy a vampire. According to a tale told by the Tlingit people of the Canadian Yukon, the sister of the Tlingit chief had tried and failed for years to have a baby when she miraculously found herself pregnant. However, it soon became clear that this was not a normal pregnancy, because the baby grew so rapidly that it was born after just a few weeks.

After birth the boy continued to grow quickly, developing sharp, pointed teeth and a body totally covered with hair. Soon people in the community began vanishing, and it was whispered that the strange boy was responsible for killing them and drinking their blood. Although the chief tried to ignore the rumors about his nephew, it became clear that the boy would have to leave for the safety of the others. When the boy refused to go, he and the chief had an epic battle, which only ended when the chief was able to throw the creature into the fire. However, as the flames consumed his body, the boy cried out that they couldn't defeat him this easily, and that he would return to drink their blood for a thousand years.

Then, as his body burned up and a cloud of ashes floated into the sky, each ash turned into a mosquito.

Of course, the vampire that is most familiar to Western cultures is the corpse returning to life from the grave and drinking the blood of its victims. Vampires from numerous eastern European cultures, such as Poland and Romania, not only crave human blood but also need it to survive.

Causes of Misfortune

Sometimes, it is the vampire's lust for blood that is used to explain various illnesses and misfortunes. Before advancements in medical science revealed the real causes of so-called "wasting" diseases such as tuberculosis—in which the person gradually wastes away—these illnesses were thought to be the work of vampires. It was believed that vampires were slowly draining the blood, and consequently the life, out of the victim, thus accounting for their gradual but steady decline.

Thanks to its thirst for blood, the mosquito plays an important role in a vampire myth of the Tlingit people of the Canadian Yukon.

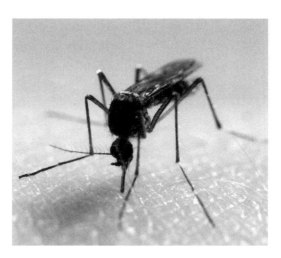

Pregnant women, new mothers, and infants were also believed to be at special risk from vampires. In Malaysia several different types of vampires menaced women and their infants in childbirth. One of the worst was the *langsuyar*, which according to myth was a once-beautiful woman whose child had been stillborn. Shocked to learn the condition of her baby, she recoiled in horror, clapped her hands, and flew into a tree. At this point she became a vampire, with ankle-length black hair that concealed an opening in her neck through which she sucked the blood of children.

The Malaysians believed that a woman who either died in childbirth or within forty days following a birth would become a *langsuyar*. To prevent this from happening, the dead woman's family placed glass beads in her mouth to silence any horrible shrieks, and eggs under her arms and needles in her palms to stop her from flying. It was also possible to turn a *langsuyar* back into a respectable member of society by cutting off her hair and long fingernails and stuffing them into the hole in her neck.

An even more horrifying Malaysian childbirth vampire was the *penanggalan*. It was said that this creature originated when a man came upon a woman performing *dudok bertapa*, a penance ceremony. Startled to see the man, the woman tried to leave but moved so abruptly and forcefully that her head separated from her body. With the stomach and intestines dangling beneath, the severed head flew into a nearby tree, becoming an evil spirit. It would appear on the rooftops of homes in which children were being born, emitting a high-pitched whine and trying to suck the blood of the newborn. The only way to stop the *penanggalan* was to place the thorny leaves of the jeruju plant around the home. The creature would not try to enter, for fear of catching its flowing entrails on the thorns.

The folklore of the Philippine Islands contains a similar creature to the *penanggalan* called the *aswang manananggal*. Like the *penanggalan*, the *aswang manananggal* was supposed to be only a head with entrails extending down from it. Like its Malaysian counterpart, it also preyed primarily on fetuses and newborns.

Indonesians had their own vampirelike creature, called a *pontianak*, to blame for babies who died at birth. The *pontianak* used her razor-sharp talons to stab a pregnant woman in the stomach and then sucked the viscera of the unborn child.

In India when crops would fail, livestock sicken, and/or illness strike people, it was often considered the work of the vampirelike *bhuta*. Thought to be the unhappy souls of men who died in an untimely manner, the *bhuta* were flicking lights or ghostly apparitions that hovered above the ground, casting no shadow. They were able to enter the body through its orifices and then possess it.

Besides Blood

While drinking blood is one of the main characteristics that people associate with vampires today, not all vampires are motivated by this desire. Sometimes, vampires simply visit ill fortune on their victims for no reason other than the pleasure such mischief gives them.

Hindu folklore tells of a vampirelike being called a *vetala*. These are spirits that inhabit cemeteries and reanimate corpses. The *vetala* is easily recognized because it has a human body, but its hands and feet are turned backward. Instead of drinking blood, the *vetala* enjoys playing tricks on the living.

Other vampires may occasionally drink blood, but the way they drain energy from a victim is quite different. In Gypsy folklore, the *mulo* is a vampire that is believed to have enormous sexual desires. The *mulo* returns primarily

The vampire is included in the folklore of many cultures. In this depiction from Bohemia, a man kills a vampire by plunging a red-hot iron into its heart.

Drinking the blood of humans is the primary characteristic that people today associate with vampires.

to have sex, particularly with its spouse and former lovers, and its appetite is so great that it often exhausts its human partners to the point of illness and even death. *Mulos* may ask their lovers to marry them, and they can also talk them into returning to the grave with them.

Sometimes, a vampire is much more subtle than drinking blood or exhausting its victim through excessive sexual activity. For instance, on Banks Island in the South Pacific, people tell of the *talamur*, which supposedly eats the soul or life force of a person near death or who has just died.

Good Vampires?

Although the vampire is usually portrayed as evil, there have also been reports of so-called "good" vampires in some cultures. Jesuit priest Father Francois Richard, in the seventeenth century, [tells] of one case on the Greek island of Santorin in which a local shoemaker turned into a *vrykolakas* (the Greek word for vampire) after his death. But instead of roaming about and terrorizing the local community, this vampire went only to his home. Here he fixed his children's shoes, cut wood for the fire, drew water and carried it to the house, and performed other chores to help his family.

Another story of a good *vrykolakas* concerns a farmhand who was devoted to the farmer who employed him. After the farmhand died, he was so worried that the farm would fail that he rose from the grave and continued to do his work at night.

In earlier times, these *vrykolakas* would have been viewed benignly by the local populace because they were not causing any harm, but in the case of the shoemaker and the farmhand, more contemporary beliefs about vampires changed public opinion. Christian teaching on vampires had linked the creatures to Satan. Thus the bodies of both the shoemaker and the farmhand were dug up and burned to ashes by the villagers.

Where Do Vampires Live?

In addition to the nature of vampires, where the creatures live also has varied according to local myths. For example, the Malaysian *penanggalan* lived in trees, while the *aswang manananggal* of the Philippines lived a normal life as an ordinary human by day and only became a bodiless head searching for victims at night.

Other vampires, such as the *bhuta* in India and the West Indies *loogaroo*, existed merely as tiny points of light and did not have a traditional home.

Chinese vampires could live in a variety of places. In one story, two young men who were spending the night in a pavilion alongside a lake were awakened from their slumber by the sound of singing. When they looked outside, they saw that the sound was coming from a beautiful woman. However, when they went out to investigate, they saw the woman's head hanging from a tree and knew that it was a vampire. They raced back into the pavilion with the head close behind them and slammed the door. The head began gnawing at the wood and seemed certain to break through the door when a rooster crowed, signaling that sunrise was near. With that the head rolled into the lake where it lived, and the men were saved.

Sometimes a vampire even lived in its mortal home, waiting to trap the unwary. The ancient Greeks told of a man who stopped at the house of a friend for the night. Unable to sleep, he heard the friend's wife and her mother whispering in the next room and realized from their conversation that they were vampires and that they were discussing which of the two men to devour. Ultimately the man managed to trick the two creatures, and the next day he and his friend killed them both.

How to Become a Vampire

Although where vampires live and what they do is open to debate, the question of how a vampire is created has largely been settled. Today it is believed that the only way to become a vampire is to be bitten by one. However, according to folklore, there have been numerous paths to vampirism.

One of the most common ways to become a vampire was to commit suicide. In cultures as diverse as those in Russia, Romania, China, and West Africa, suicide victims were believed to become vampires. This linkage is likely rooted in the belief that suicide was the most antisocial act that a person could commit. Since antisocial behavior was something for which vampires were widely known, it was only a small step to link suicide with vampirism.

Someone who committed suicide was considered antisocial because he or she left problems and relationships with others unresolved. Thus it was felt that the person would return after death to continue disturbing the living. Because of the link between suicide and vampirism, corpses of suicides were often denied a normal Christian burial. Corpses were sometimes even thrown into a nearby river so that they would be carried away from town and not return as vampires.

In this scene from a 1958 film, a vampire eyes the tempting neck of his victim. Many believe the only way to become a vampire is to be bitten by one.

If such precautions were not taken, vampirism could result, as this seventeenth-century tale related by philosopher Henry More illustrates. It seems that a shoemaker killed himself by cutting his own throat, but the family hid this fact from the authorities and the man was given a proper Christian burial. Soon, however, rumors about the suicide came out. The man's wife threatened legal action against anyone who advocated digging up her husband's corpse, so people were silenced.

However, human law could not compete with supernatural law, and soon there were reports of a foul specter in the form of the shoemaker that was attacking people in the town. Eventually the body was dug up, and all present were astonished to see that there were no signs of decomposition, despite the body's having been in the earth for eight months. The body was left aboveground while the authorities pondered what to do, and during that time the shoemaker began to attack members of his own family. At last his wife admitted the circumstances of his death and said that she would not stand in the way of further action against the vampire. Authorities promptly cut off the shoemaker's arms and legs, removed his heart, and burned everything. They then put the ashes in a sack that they threw into a river, and they were not troubled anymore by the vampire shoemaker.

Another way that a corpse could become a vampire was if a cat jumped over it prior to burial. For this reason, the Chinese and the Greeks were particularly watchful of corpses laid out in the home before burial. Why cats were thought to have this power is unclear, but in many parts of Europe, at least, cats were traditionally believed to be in league with Satan.

To Remain Indissoluble

Once Christian beliefs were incorporated into beliefs about vampires, excommunication became a surefire path to vampirism. A person who was excommunicated from the Church had been cast out of God's favor and thus was easily controlled by the devil. The excommunication service always ended with the priest declaring that the body of the person being cast out would, after death, "remain indissoluble."[1] In fact, this part of the rite of excommunication was the basis for the belief that any body that did not decay in the ground was a vampire. The horror that a disinterred body could evoke among the living certainly would have lent credence to the belief that Satan was somehow involved. One body that was disinterred and found not to have decomposed was described as follows:

The skin was distended, hard, and livid, and so swollen everywhere that the body had no flat surfaces but was round like a full sack. The face was covered with hair dark and curly; on the head there was little hair, as also on the rest of the body, which appeared smooth all over; the arms by reason of the swelling of the corpse were stretched out on each side like the arms of a cross; the hands were open, the eyelids closed, the mouth gaping, and the teeth white.[2]

This concept became so ingrained that in the eighteenth century the Greek Orthodox Church, concerned about losing souls to vampires, insisted that all bodies be dug up after three years. If a body was found to not have decomposed, then it was considered a *vrykolakas* and a tool of the devil.

Christians believed that a body that did not decay after burial was a vampire.

As for the bite of a vampire turning a victim into such a creature, this is rarely mentioned in traditional folklore. Initially, vampires fed on their prey for an extended period of time, and the usual result was death for the victim. This reflects the vampire's connection with wasting diseases. Researchers are uncertain when it became common to believe that the bite from a vampire turned the victim into a vampire. According to a Greek monk's account from the late 1880s, vampires increase their numbers through this method, but this seems to be an isolated report.

How to Find and Destroy a Vampire

The route to becoming a vampire is shrouded in mystery. Similarly, the problem of how to find and kill a creature that is undead is one that has bedeviled vampire hunters in eastern Europe for centuries.

Of course, before a vampire could be killed it must be found, and this was more difficult than one might imagine. In ancient times, vampires sometimes masqueraded as legitimate members of society and therefore were extremely difficult to unmask until they did something to reveal their true nature.

Once vampires came to be thought of as inhabiting cemeteries, finding them became a bit easier. If a vampire was thought to be at work, the first victim of an epidemic was usually the logical suspect to have become a vampire. Once this person's grave was found and opened, the vampire was destroyed.

However, if the identity of the vampire was unknown, there were several methods that could be used to uncover it. One of these was to scatter ash or salt—which vampires were thought to avoid—around all the graves; in the morning, the grave with the footprints around it would be the home of the vampire. Another procedure was to lead a pure white or black horse around the graveyard. Supposedly,

such coloring was an indication of spiritual purity, and the horse would naturally avoid stepping on or over the grave of such an impure creature as a vampire. Having a virgin boy astride the horse added another level of purity and virtually guaranteed the discovery of the vampire's grave. Other possible dwelling places of vampires were graves where the ground had sunk in or developed holes. Graves with crooked crosses or tombstones were also suspect.

People came to believe that vampires inhabited cemeteries. Graves with crooked tombstones were suspected to harbor such creatures.

Ways to Kill a Vampire

Finding a vampire, of course, only solved half the problem. Once discovered, the creature had to be destroyed so that it could no longer return to menace the living.

The time-honored way to kill a vampire was to drive a stake through its heart. Usually the stake was made of wood; aspen was the preferred choice, although ash, hawthorn, maple, blackthorn, or whitethorn could be substituted.

Sometimes iron stakes were used in place of wood. Long needles or nails could be substituted for stakes.

Once a preventive measure, staking a corpse dates back to before the use of coffins for burials became common. According to tradition, the stake pinned the body to the ground, thereby preventing it from leaving its grave. Eventually, the practice of staking came to be thought of as a means not of preventing vampirism, but of ending it.

Still, there were other ways to kill a vampire. For example, a vampire could also be killed by decapitation. This was a method commonly used throughout Germany and countries of eastern Europe. It was believed that removing the head prevented it from directing the body to do its evil bidding. Typically the corpse was removed from its grave, decapitated, and staked.

Those who decapitated the corpses took no chances. In some countries, such as Poland, after the head was removed, it was placed between the corpse's knees or underneath an arm, thus making it more difficult to rejoin the body. Sometimes the head was buried separately, so that it could never return to its body. As an additional precaution, the severed head was sometimes stuffed with coins, garlic, or stones.

While usually removal of the head by any means was satisfactory, in some Slavic cultures tradition dictated that only a shovel belonging to either a sexton (essentially a church's custodian) or a grave digger could be used for this purpose. A grave digger's shovel was thought to contain special qualities that would make the vampire stay in its grave because the shovel was constantly in touch with cemetery ground; a sexton's shovel was effective because it was thought to be infused with the power of God.

However, if the vampire was persistent and continued to be a problem even after being staked and decapitated, the one sure way to destroy the creature was to burn its body. Cremation, however, presented problems. The human body is more than 70 percent water, making it fire resistant. A body will eventually burn, but only on the side exposed to air. Moreover, wood fires typically could not generate enough heat to reduce a body to ash. Chopping the corpse into small pieces solved these problems even though doing so required considerable strength on the part of the man wielding the ax.

Ways to Prevent a Vampire Attack

Sometimes people found themselves in situations where they lacked the means to kill a vampire but still needed to do something to stop the creature from attacking. Folklore provides numerous methods to prevent vampire attacks.

Many believed that burning a vampire was the only sure way of destroying the creature.

One of the best ways to fend off a vampire was to use garlic, either by hanging it by the window or door or wearing a wreath made of it. It is unclear why vampires should fear garlic, but this herb has been considered a powerful healing agent since ancient times. Moreover, garlic has a reputation in many cultures, such as European, South American, Chinese, and Mexican, as a deterrent against evil.

Another method used to foil a vampire away was to turn the creature's tendency toward compulsive neatness against it. Legend had it that throwing a handful of seeds, salt, or sand into the path of a vampire would force it to stop and pick up every single granule before continuing its pursuit. The same objects could also be spread around the bed to stop or at least slow down a vampire that was threatening a sleeping person. In later years a newspaper came to be used in this same way: According to legend, a vampire that encounters a newspaper must stop and read every word.

Other popular protections against vampires were religious items such as crosses, crucifixes, and bottles of holy water. If all else failed, however, and the vampire attacked, a victim lucky enough to have a knife made of silver handy could wound the creature.

While these were the most popular ways to defeat a vampire, the Chinese had a few additional methods for warding off such creatures. According to one story, an artist was sketching a memorial portrait of a friend's dead father when the corpse suddenly sat up. Realizing that the corpse was a vampire, the artist called down to men from the undertaker's establishment to hurry upstairs and bring brooms. The men arrived just in time and used the brooms to keep the vampire at bay until it could be locked in its coffin.

Another Chinese tale concerns a vampire that was attacking a mountain village. In desperation the people asked a priest for help. He gave a young man from the village copper bells, explaining that the sound from such

In this scene from the 1958 movie Dracula, *a vampire is rendered helpless at the sight of a cross.*

instruments renders evil creatures powerless. When night fell and the vampire came out of his cave, the young man began ringing his copper bells. The sound put the vampire into a type of hypnotic trance, during which all it could do was glare at the young man. The youth kept ringing the bells until dawn, when the vampire fell dead.

Vampire legends from other cultures notwithstanding, as the eighteenth century ended, the Western world's image of the vampire had crystallized into a creature that emerged from its grave during the night to terrorize the living. But this was far different from the ways vampires had originally been portrayed.

Chapter 2

A Creature from the Mists of Time

The modern-day concept of a vampire as a creature that rises from the grave to seek human blood is a merging of two powerful ideas that have existed almost since the beginning of humankind: fear of the dead returning to life and the importance of blood.

Respect the Dead

From before recorded history, people have taken elaborate measures to make sure that the dead are treated with respect. In many cultures, this was done because it was believed that the soul of a dead person remained powerful and would return to wreak vengeance on the living if it was unhappy.

Just when people began to think of these vengeful souls as vampires is uncertain. What is known is that early on the living began to take precautions to see that the dead remained content—and that they stayed put in their graves. This is why the nomads of ancient Scythia (which encompassed parts of modern-day southeast Europe and central Asia) buried dead kings with the bodies of those who could serve them in the afterlife: servants, a cook, groom, valet,

and even their favorite concubine. Just to be certain that a deceased king remained happy (and in the ground), one year after his death, fifty of his servants and fifty of his best horses would be killed. After stuffing the bodies with straw, the tribe would mount a servant atop each horse and place the animals standing guard over the king's grave.

Actor Tom Cruise portrays a vampire about to drain the blood from his victim in the 1994 movie Interview with the Vampire.

Other cultures followed similar rituals to pacify their dead. African tribes built temples for dead kings and killed some of their followers so that they could serve their master in death. They also periodically brought food to the grave and dropped it through a specially built hole that led to where the bodies were buried so that the dead would have enough to eat and not feel compelled to return to the world of the living.

The Blood Is the Life

People from diverse cultures also realized the importance that blood played in sustaining life. Around the world, rituals that involved the draining of blood from the living abounded. The ancient Romans, for example, practiced a

The Romans offered blood to the god Attis (seated, center) to ensure fertility of the soil.

ceremony in which they offered their blood to Attis, the god of vegetation, to ensure the fertility of their soil.

In a similar ceremony, the Aztecs of ancient Mexico annually held a bloody and violent celebration designed to resurrect Chicomecohuatl, their maize (corn) goddess. A young virgin, adorned with a wreath on her head and a corncob necklace, would dance at the goddess's temple throughout the entire night. A large group of worshipers danced around her, cutting themselves, collecting the blood in small basins, and offering it to her. At the first light of dawn, the high priest cut off the girl's head; the lesser priests scrambled to catch the blood, which they used to fertilize the fields. The Aztecs hoped that this blood sacrifice would appease and rejuvenate Chicomecohuatl.

Other cultures, such as the ancient Carthaginians and Gauls, took the belief in blood's mystic power a step further. They believed that by drinking the blood of dead enemies, they would absorb their foes' heroic qualities.

In Australia the Aborigines considered blood a vital ingredient in curing the sick. When a person became ill, their family would find a willing donor and collect some of the blood in a wooden bowl. When the blood had hardened into a jellylike state, the sick person would consume it in the hope that the healthy, life-giving properties of the donor's blood would help speed recovery.

A Convergence of Beliefs

With the life-giving power of blood so clearly evident, perhaps it was inevitable that some people linked this idea with the notion of the dead returning to life. According to this logic, a corpse that sought to live again would certainly need human blood, the essential fluid of life, to sustain its existence.

Once these beliefs merged, it was only a short step to the creation of the mythological creature known as the vampire. Contributing to the belief in vampires was the need of people to attribute events that they did not understand, such as death from certain diseases like tuberculosis, to supernatural entities. In particular, illnesses that were characterized by the gradual weakening of the victim were often blamed on vampires.

However, although these vampires shared the characteristics of returning from the dead and drinking their victims' blood, their exact form and how they went about their gruesome business still varied, depending upon the culture from which they sprang.

Vampires in Various Forms

Although in Western imaginations vampires ultimately became almost exclusively reanimated human corpses, this

In past centuries, ignorance about the causes of illness and death contributed to the belief in vampires.

was not always the case in the creature's early history. In Greek mythology there is a vampirelike spirit called an *empusai*, which had no shape of its own but could invade the body of a person and then use him or her for its own evil purposes. In the *Life of Apollonius of Tyana* by Philostratus, Apollonius saves his friend Menippus from marrying a beautiful woman who was in fact an *empusai* and who was only marrying Menippus so that she could devour him and drink his blood.

Another vampire that menaced the Greeks was the *lamia*. According to the myth, there was once a Libyan queen named Lamia who had children by Zeus, the king of the gods. In a fit of jealousy, Zeus's wife Hera stole the children from Lamia. Unable to retaliate against Hera because she was too powerful, Lamia took refuge in a cave and took out her revenge on all children by sucking their blood. Eventually Lamia became the name of a group of female demons. Although the *lamia* still primarily attacked young children, they also had the power to transform themselves into beautiful young women. In this form they seduced and attacked young men.

Another vampire in Greek folklore is the *strige*, a nocturnal demon that preyed on young children. The *strige* found its way into Roman folklore as well. The Roman poet Ovid wrote about them:

> Voracious birds there are . . . that fly forth by night and assail children who still need a nurse's care, and seize them out of their cradles, and do them mischief. With their beaks they are said to pick out the child's milk-fed bowels, and their throat is full of the blood they drink. *Striges* they are called.[3]

The Tale of Lilith

The ancient Babylonians believed in a wide range of vampire demons. One of the most famous was Lilith, a vampire harlot who was unable to have children. Because she came to be identified with the night, she was often portrayed as a beautiful young woman with the feet of an owl.

The early Hebrews incorporated Lilith into their beliefs and changed her origin to that of Adam's first wife (before Eve). According to the legend, after an argument over sex, Lilith left Adam and flew to the Red Sea, where she acquired a range of evil powers. She then returned to haunt and torment Adam and Eve, causing them to create inhuman offspring. Since Lilith's demonic origin had its roots in a disagreement about sex, she was said to hate the human children that were produced by the normal mating of men and women, and she would try to kill newborns by sucking their blood and strangling them.

According to Babylonian and Hebrew myths, Lilith was a vampire demon who killed human babies.

Vampires in Chinese Folklore

China also had a strong vampire tradition. It stemmed from the Chinese belief in two souls: The *hun* is the superior or rational soul, while the *p'ai* is the inferior or irrational soul. It was the *p'ai* that could lead to vampirism, because it could linger in a dead body before it was buried; if the *p'ai* was strong enough, it could reanimate the body and make it function like a living person. This was called a *chiang-shih*, or vampire. Because the body appeared normal, a *chiang-shih* was often impossible to detect until it did something that gave away its true identity. However, sometimes the *chiang-shih* became quite hideous, developing serrated teeth and long talons and emitting an eerie green glow. Fortunately the power of the *p'ai* was limited, and it could not resurrect a body once it was safely in the ground. With this in mind, the Chinese rushed to bury their dead.

The *chiang-shih* exhibited several traits that would ultimately become part of the vampire tradition elsewhere. Likely candidates to become vampires were suicide victims, as well as any person who suffered a particularly violent or untimely death. In addition, the Chinese vampire could only operate at night. Finally, the *chiang-shih* had great difficulty crossing running water. All of these characteristics would later find their way into Western vampire folklore.

The Vampire Moves West

Fear of the dead returning to attack the living was a trait common to many cultures, and thus as civilization developed throughout Europe and Great Britain, so too did belief in vampires. However, in Western mythology a vampire gradually came to be seen solely as a reanimated corpse. In achieving this transition, the vampire was aided, ironically, by organized Christian religion.

The Church and Vampires

As Christianity spread across Europe, it found many obstacles in its way. Superstition, folk beliefs, and remnants of pagan religions all vied with the Church for influence.

In vampires and other demons, the Church saw an opportunity to gain the upper hand over the competing beliefs. The Church felt that if it could establish itself as the only institution able to defeat such creatures, people would naturally gravitate to it. Thus, instead of downplaying the belief in vampires as merely products of superstitious ignorance, the Church encouraged it—with one important difference. Instead of portraying vampires simply as evil creatures whose origins came from a variety of sources and causes, vampires were all portrayed as minions of Satan. This made the dividing line between the two sides crystal clear: The Church stood for God and righteousness, while vampires stood for the devil and evil. Since the Church was the only force powerful enough to combat Satan, by extension it became the only force powerful enough to defeat vampires.

This harnessing of belief in vampires to its own purposes represented a reversal of Christian doctrine. Initially, the Church had dismissed vampires, witches, and other demons as simply the unenlightened remnants of pagan beliefs. But once the Church could use belief in vampires to their advantage, this view gradually changed until, in 1215, the Church formally acknowledged the existence of vampires during the Fourth Lateran Council of Catholic Church leaders in Rome.

By that time, however, most people needed little official encouragement to believe in vampires; they were certain that they were real. It was not only uneducated peasants who feared and believed in such creatures; learned men were also documenting cases of apparent vampirism. In the

Early Church leaders perpetuated the belief that vampires were all minions of Satan.

35

twelfth century, for example, Walter Map, archdeacon of Oxford, related numerous incidents of the dead coming back to terrorize the living.

One of Map's reports concerned a soldier who appealed to the bishop of Hereford for help in stopping a dead man who continually appeared before the house in which the soldier lived. The dead man would call out the name of a lodger in the house, and inevitably that person would die within a few days. Realizing that it was only a matter of time until the dead man got to his name, the soldier appealed to the bishop for help. Following church doctrine, the bishop determined that these woes were caused by "an evil angel of that accursed wretch [Satan], so that he is able to rouse himself and walk abroad in his dead body."[4] Eventually, with the bishop's help, the soldier killed the vampire.

Even more shocking were a series of occurrences documented around this time by another church official in England, Canon William of Newburgh in his *Historia Rerum Anglicarum*, also called the *Chronicles*. Chapters 32 through 34 of the book contain numerous tales of vampire activity in the British Isles at such respected places as Alnwick Castle and Melrose Abbey.

William was a careful chronicler of events, and he knew that other scholars might greet his reports with skepticism. Thus he sought to strengthen their believability by writing:

> It is, I am very well aware, quite true that unless they were amply supported by many examples which have taken place in our own days, and by the unimpeachable testimony of responsible persons, these facts would not easily be believed, to wit, that the bodies of the dead may arise from their tombs and that vitalized by some supernatural power, they speed hither and thither, either greatly alarming or in some cases actually slaying the living, and when

Melrose Abbey in Scotland was one location noted in William of Newburgh's twelfth-century book, Chronicles, *as a site of vampire activity.*

they return to the grave it seems to open to them of their own accord.[5]

The Church Miscalculates

The fact that distinguished men like William of Newburgh were giving credence to vampires tended to reinforce the belief among the peasantry that such creatures were real. By tapping into the age-old fear of the dead returning to life, the Church unwittingly amplified it; now, those who formerly might have been ridiculed for their belief in such things had merely to point to the Church's position on the matter. It became very easy to blame any type of illness or sudden, mysterious death on vampires. Buoyed by the Church's blessing, belief in vampires spread rapidly throughout Europe.

Helping spur this belief along were the continuing bouts of bubonic plague that periodically swept through Europe from the fourteenth through the eighteenth century. Swift in its spread and deadly, the plague exacted a horrifying toll across the European continent. (For example, during the outbreak of plague known as the Black Death from 1347 to 1351, Europe lost approximately one-third of its population.)

A man carries a sick child through the streets of London during the Black Death.

With just a rudimentary knowledge of medicine, doctors were helpless against the plague. Unable to contain or cure the disease, people quickly attributed the thousands of deaths it caused to supernatural entities, including vampires. The fact that plague victims often wasted away, just as supposedly happened to those upon whom vampires fed, added to the conviction that vampires were involved.

Even educated men agreed that vampires were hard at work during the Black Death. William of Newburgh related a story about how the decomposing body of a vampire from Berwick fouled the air all about him and brought a plague that practically wiped out the entire town.

A Serious Matter

By the seventeenth century, vampirism was considered such a serious matter by the Church that books were written by religious scholars on how to deal with the problem. In 1645 scholar, physician, and theologian Leo Allatius wrote what some modern-day researchers consider the first modern book on vampires, entitled *De Graecorum hodie quorundam opinationibus* (On the Current Opinions of Certain Greeks). Although in it Leo Allatius primarily discusses vampires, known as *vrykolakas* in his native Greece, he also firmly identified vampires as minions of the devil.

In his book Allatius even goes so far as to link vampires to witches by adapting guidelines used for identifying witches to apply to vampires. These guidelines specify that witchcraft requires the presence of a devil and a witch, along with the permission of God. Allatius writes that the same is true for vampires, except that he replaced "a witch" with "a dead body." Allatius's guidelines gave added credibility to ideas about vampires. Since scores of witches had supposedly been identified using these criteria, the very fact that someone would use these same criteria to identify vampires meant that they must also exist.

The Fear Spreads

Other works soon followed in which scholars and religious leaders tried to understand and explain vampirism. In 1653 Henry More, a Christian philosopher in Cambridge, England, published his history of vampires, *An Appeal to the Natural Faculties of the Mind of Man, whether there be not a God*. In it he contends that anyone who commits suicide will become a vampire.

With all of these authoritative assertions of the existence of vampires, many coming from leaders in the Catholic Church, it was perhaps inevitable that a wave of vampire incidents should be reported. Beginning in the late 1600s and continuing well into the following century, a

In the seventeenth century, Church leaders believed that witchcraft required the presence of a witch and a devil, pictured here. Leo Allatius, a scholar writing at the time, applied these guidelines to vampirism, substituting "a dead body" for "a witch."

flood of reports of vampire sightings and attacks, and of subsequent efforts to destroy these creatures, surged out of eastern Europe, particularly Prussia and Poland, where the Roman Catholic Church was dominant.

The Case of Arnold Paole

The best-known case concerns Arnold Paole, who lived in the village of Medvegia in Austria in 1726. A former soldier who had become a farmer, Paole was an honest, hardworking man with a gloomy manner. He finally told his fiancée that the reason he was depressed was that he had been attacked by a vampire while in the army. Although he had hunted down the creature and killed it, and also had eaten some of the dirt from its grave and bathed his wounds in its blood, he was afraid that these precautions were not enough and that he would turn into a vampire upon his death.

Ironically, soon after this Paole died. A few weeks later, people began seeing him around the village. Four of the people who reported seeing Paole subsequently died. Certain that he had become a vampire and was responsible for the deaths, the townspeople dug up his body. When the coffin was opened, his body was found to not have suffered any decomposition at all; the hair and beard appeared to be still growing, and blood was trickling from the mouth. Even more horrifying was the fact that when Paole's body was pierced, blood oozed forth. It was immediately concluded that Paole was a vampire. This conclusion was reinforced when a stake was driven through his heart and the corpse emitted a loud groan. To stop Paole's attacks, his head was cut off and the body burned. The bodies of the four people who had died were treated in a similar fashion to prevent them from returning as vampires as well.

The people of Medvegia thought that they had taken care of their vampire problem, but five years later it began all over again. In 1731, within three months seventeen people died in violent and mysterious ways that the town leaders concluded could only be attributed to a vampire. Furthermore, a girl reported that a man named Milo, who had recently died, had attacked her one night.

When word of this latest outbreak of vampire activity reached Vienna, capital of Austria, regimental field surgeon Dr. Johannes Fluckinger was appointed to investigate the situation. Arriving at Medvegia, the doctor found that the people believed so strongly that vampires were the cause of the deaths that they would accept nothing less than disinterring the bodies of those under suspicion. In all, forty bodies were dug up under Fluckinger's supervision; seventeen were found not to have decomposed and so were staked, decapitated, and burned.

Fluckinger's report to the Vienna authorities about the Medvegia vampires was widely publicized across Europe and England. A rash of incidents in which supposed vampires were dug up and dispatched followed. The following description of the treatment given to the corpse of a suspected vampire was typical:

> They [village officials] cut off the Head, Arms, and Legs of the Corpse, and opening his Back, took out his Heart, which was as fresh and Intire as a Calf new-killed. These, together with his body, they put on a pile of wood, together, and burnt them to Ashes, which they carefully sweeping together, and putting in a Sack (that none might get them for Wicked uses) poured them into the River, after which the Spectrum [vampire] was never seen more.[6]

The Church Tries to Reverse Its Course

Church officials were very concerned by accounts of what had happened in Medvegia, as well as other reports of vampire activity elsewhere in Europe. Church doctrine held that the bodies of those who had received Christian burial were awaiting resurrection and must be kept intact;

Digging up bodies to determine if they were vampires became common as fear of the creatures grew.

the knowledge that these bodies were being dug up, mutilated, and in some cases burned by fearful vampire-hunting villagers was therefore horrifying to church officials. The events that the Church had set in motion so many centuries ago by fostering a belief in vampires had now come back to threaten one of the basic tenets of Christian faith.

Church officials, alarmed at the damage they had unwittingly done to innocent Christians, belatedly began telling their followers that lack of decomposition in a body did not necessarily mean that the person had become a vampire. Churchmen also besieged the Catholic leadership in Rome with inquiries about how to handle the growing reports of vampires and the resulting desecration of corpses. In response, in 1738 respected Italian archbishop Giuseppe Davanzati was assigned to investigate the reports of vampires and determine the Church's response.

Davanzati spent several years sifting through all the accounts of vampire activity. When issued in 1744, his report concluded that vampires were not real but originated in human fantasies, although he allowed that some of these fantasies might be due to the influence of Satan. He recommended that even the bodies of suspected vampires

Shocked that bodies were being disinterred and dismembered in the fight against vampires, Church leaders insisted that those who received Christian burial remain undisturbed.

should remain undisturbed. This became the Church's official position on vampires.

In his report, Davanzati also had scathing words for those who believed in vampires. "Why is this demon so partial to baseborn plebeians [commoners]?" he asked.

> Why is it always peasants, carters, shoemakers, and innkeepers? Why has the demon never been known to assume the form of a man of quality, a scholar, a philosopher, a theologian, a magnate or a bishop? I will tell you why: learned men and men of quality are not so easily deceived as idiots and men of low birth and therefore do not so easily allow themselves to be taken in by appearances.[7]

Calmet's Report

The Church hoped that Davanzati's decision would help put an end to the belief in vampires and the destruction of corpses. Unfortunately, Davanzati's report did not receive as much publicity as one written around the same time by a French Roman Catholic biblical scholar named Don Augustin Calmet. Calmet also examined hundreds of cases of reported vampirism, focusing on many of the physical questions that bothered him and other learned men about the subject. For example, if a vampire was a spectral entity, how could it suck the blood of the living? Or, how could a vampire leave and reenter its grave without disturbing the earth? "We are enmeshed in a sad dilemma when we ask if these apparitions are natural or miraculous,"[8] he writes.

Just as compelling to Calmet was the reason vampires existed at all. If, he postulated, vampires were truly dead people returned to life, then they must be animated by demons, which could only happen with God's permission. Thus he saw a paradox: God, the greatest force for goodness in the world, was responsible for unleashing one of the most incredible forces of evil in the world. Why God did that was a mystery that puzzled Calmet, although he was not inclined to delve into it further. He explains:

> We must then keep silence on this article, since it has not pleased God to reveal to us either the extent of the demon's power, or the way in which these things can be done. We may easily console ourselves for our ignorance in that respect, since there are so many natural things which take place within us and around us, of which the cause and manner are unknown to us.[9]

Calmet was deeply skeptical of the existence of vampires—at one point he labeled the many tales he had heard as "utterly without foundation . . . absurd and contradictory"[10]—but he also was unable to find natural explanations for them, calling the subject difficult and mysterious. Thus he left the entire matter up to others to find the truth.

However, despite not coming to a definitive conclusion, Calmet revealed his own feelings when he wrote:

> It seems impossible not to subscribe to the belief which prevails in these countries that these apparitions do actually come forth from the graves and that they are able to produce the terrible effects which are so widely and so positively attributed to them.[11]

Because of its ambiguous conclusion, Calmet's book produced a storm of criticism. Skeptics assailed him for giving legitimacy to what they considered little more than stories designed to frighten children. The book, however, became a best-seller and was translated into both German and English. The criticism bothered Calmet, and in a subsequent edition he concluded that vampires did not exist. However, it was too late to save his reputation—and also too late to undo what many saw as an authoritative endorsement of the existence of vampires.

Empress Maria Theresa of Austria transferred authority over vampire cases to her central government in an unsuccessful attempt to end the rampant exhumation and destruction of corpses.

Laws Have No Effect

Faced with the failure of Davanzati's report in quashing belief in vampires and the resulting desecration of corpses, the Church pressured government officials to pass laws that would prevent such mutilation. In 1755 and 1756 Empress Maria Theresa of Austria enacted measures that transferred authority for handling vampire cases from parish priests and local officials to the central government. It was hoped that this would curtail the feverish exhumation and destruction of suspected vampire corpses occurring in Austria at this time.

But the new regulations were to no avail. Fearful peasants in remote villages far from the influence of the central government were not about to let any new laws stop them from disposing of vampires. Bodies continued to be dug up, mutilated, and even burned when the situation called for it.

However, little could anyone know that the image of a vampire as the reanimated corpse of a European peasant was about to undergo a radical transformation—thanks to a group of friends and their desire for entertainment.

Chapter 3

Vampires in Popular Culture

The transformation of the image of a vampire from that of a European peasant wearing simple clothing to that of a stylishly dressed aristocrat occurred early in the nineteenth century—the result of an encounter between several giants of English literature and some inclement weather.

Inspiration from the Storm

Late in the spring of 1816, the famous English poet and writer Lord George Gordon Byron arrived in Geneva, Switzerland, during a tour of Europe. With him was a young physician and writer named John Polidori. The two men rented the Villa Diodati, overlooking Lake Geneva. Soon they were joined by Byron's fellow poet Percy Bysshe Shelley, writer Mary Wollstonecraft (soon to be Shelley's wife), and Claire Clairmont, Byron's mistress.

On June 15 a fierce storm forced the group to remain indoors. To relieve their boredom, Byron suggested that each person write a ghost story that would be read to the others.

Byron produced an incomplete short story about two men, just like he and Polidori, who were traveling in

Lord Byron's suggestion that he and his friends invent ghost stories to pass the time one night led to the first published story about a vampire.

Europe. One of the men is mortally injured and makes his friend promise to keep his death a secret. The friend agrees, only to discover when he returns to England that not only is the supposedly dead man alive but that he is dating his sister.

Byron saw no future in the story and abandoned it. But Polidori took careful notes on Byron's story when the writer read it to the group. Shortly thereafter the two men parted company; Byron continued traveling while Polidori returned to England.

"The Vampyre"

Once back in England, Polidori took Byron's plot and developed it into a short story called "The Vampyre," which was published in the April 1819 edition of *New Monthly Magazine*. In the story, a rich young Englishman named Aubrey travels to Greece with the mysterious and aristocratic Lord Ruthven, whom he had met in London. While in Greece the two men are attacked by bandits; Ruthven is mortally wounded but gets Aubrey to swear that he will tell no one of his death. When Aubrey returns to England, he finds that Ruthven—not dead at all—is also there. Unable to tell anyone of Ruthven's supposed death because of his promise, Aubrey suffers a nervous breakdown while Ruthven begins dating and ultimately is engaged to marry Aubrey's sister. In the end Ruthven, who is revealed as a vampire only in the last line of the story, kills Aubrey's sister and disappears, while Aubrey dies from nervous exhaustion brought about by the stress of keeping his promise.

"The Vampyre" created a sensation in London literary circles, partly because it was erroneously published under Byron's name. Polidori had told the editor of *New Monthly Magazine* how the story had originated, and the editor himself decided to put Byron's name on it. Byron cleared up the misunderstanding, and eventually Polidori received full credit for the story.

Breaking New Ground

What made Polidori's story so important in the history of English literature was the portrayal of the vampire as an independent-thinking entity. Polidori transformed the vampire from a European peasant who returns from the grave to wreak mindless vengeance into a sinister nobleman who carefully plans his evil actions. Previously, the vampire known to Europeans attacked whomever and whatever it encountered; the vampire created by Polidori carefully chose his victims, demonstrating cunning and intelligence that heretofore had not been portrayed in vampiric folklore. As J. Gordon Melton, author of *The Vampire Book*, writes: "[The vampire] was not an impersonal evil entity but a moral degenerate dominated by evil motives, and a subject about whom negative moral judgments were proper."[12]

One of the reasons that Polidori most likely changed the vampire character into a nobleman is that he was writing for an audience of his peers—upper-crust aristocrats who would have had little interest in a story about a European peasant. Another reason is that the plot hinges on

Writer John Polidori's vampire was depicted as a sinister and intelligent nobleman, establishing a literary convention that continues to this day, as in actor Frank Langella's portrayal in the 1979 film, Dracula.

the idea that a gentleman always keeps his word. Today the notion that a person would remain silent if he or she knew that a family member was in terrible danger is not believable, but in Polidori's day it was a time-honored tradition, especially among members of the upper class, that a promise is meant to be kept, no matter what the consequences.

Neither Polidori nor Byron lived to see the legacy created by their unintentional collaboration on the landmark vampire tale. Polidori committed suicide in 1821 at the age of twenty-six, and Byron died three years later, at age thirty-six. But because of its popularity, "The Vampyre" caused an explosion in vampire literature; stories, poems, and plays about vampires quickly became common fare in England, France, and Germany. The character of Lord Ruthven also enjoyed widespread notoriety; in 1820 he appeared in four plays about vampires in Paris alone—two serious and two comedic. For the next thirty years, Ruthven remained a staple of vampire literature. Even the noted French writer Alexandre Dumas (author of *The Three Musketeers* and *The Count of Monte Cristo*) felt sufficiently stimulated by the character of Ruthven to feature him in the last play the famous author ever wrote, *Le Vampire*, in 1851.

Varney the Vampire

With all of the attention given to Lord Ruthven, it took more than twenty years for another important vampire character to emerge, but when he did he was as different from Ruthven as anyone might imagine. In the mid-1840s Varney the vampire appeared as the main character in a series of 109 weekly installments published under the title *Varney the Vampyre, or The Feast of Blood*. Eventually all of the installments were collected and published in 1847 in a novel that totaled over eight hundred pages in length. As such, *Varney the Vampire* is considered the first full-length vampire novel published in the English language.

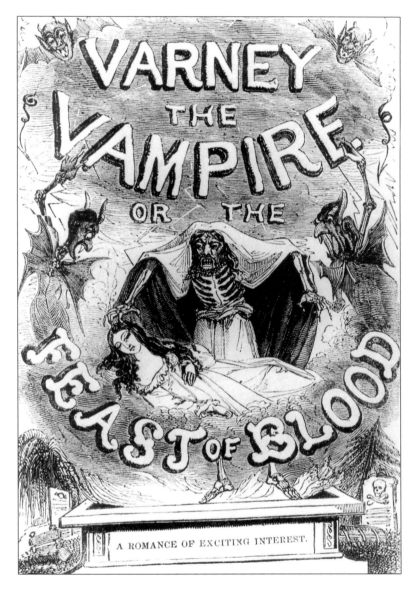

Varney the Vampire, or The Feast of Blood *was the first full-length vampire novel published in English.*

Primarily written by Scottish-born author James Malcolm Rymer, *Varney the Vampire* is also different from Polidori's story in that it was literature intended for the working class. Polidori's story was written for and about high society; the story's style is calm and reserved, almost like the conversation at a fancy dinner party.

This illustration from the 1847 novel, Varney the Vampire, *shows Varney with one of his victims.*

Varney, on the other hand, was written for what was then considered to be the far less discriminating tastes of the lower classes. The story was meant to excite and titillate the reader so that he or she would buy the next installment. Thus the writing in each installment was explicit, with plenty of action, thrills, and horror jammed into its pages. The following paragraph from the first chapter, in which Varney invades a woman's bedroom, illustrates the frenzied writing style of *Varney*:

> The glassy, horrible eyes of the figure [Varney] ran over that angelic form with a hideous satisfaction—horrible profanation. He drags her head to the bed's edge. He forces it back by the long hair still entwined in his grasp. With a plunge he seizes the neck in his fang-like teeth—a gush of blood, and a hideous sucking noise follows. The girl has swooned, and the vampyre is at his hideous repast![13]

While *Varney* was not a great step forward for English literature, its popularity reinforced ideas about vampires that Polidori had introduced. Like Ruthven, Varney was extremely strong, walked around during the day, and only needed to occasionally feed to survive. Although he could be wounded and even killed, simply lying in the light of the moon would restore him to health. (This is also how Ruthven returned to life in Polidori's story.)

Other Types of Vampires

Meanwhile, both before and after publication of *Varney the Vampyre*, writers incorporated vampires into their work. While many were content to keep them as blood-drinking monsters, others sought new ways of exploring the vampire theme. Energy-draining vampires (those that feed off a person's energy and life force, rather than blood) first appeared in 1853 in Charles Wilkins Webber's novel *Spiritual Vampirism*. In both Smyth Upton's *The Last of the Vampires* and G. W. M. Reynolds's *Faust*, vampirism is presented as a type of magic formula, in which the vampire obtains power and continued life in exchange for serving dark forces.

Another milestone in the vampire legend occurred at this time when women began to be portrayed as vampires. Most writers had used males as their vampire character, partly because it allowed them to cloak their stories in an aura of sexuality that would never have been allowed in other types of literature. In *Varney*, for example, the vampire's repeated attacks on women are suggestive of forced sexual conquest and rape—both taboo subjects in literature at the time.

"Carmilla"

However, by focusing on women as vampires, writers were also able to introduce another type of heretofore forbidden sexuality into their stories: lesbianism. This theme can clearly be seen in "Carmilla," published in 1872. Written by Irish-born Joseph Thomas Sheridan Le Fanu, "Carmilla" tells the story of a young woman named Laura, who is visited by the vampire Carmilla in her bed late at night. Laura's fear of her nocturnal visitor is soon overpowered by her sensual attraction to Carmilla, who climbs into bed with the girl and lightly kisses and caresses her until she falls asleep.

Laura gradually weakens from Carmilla's continued visits. Just in time the vampire's true identity is discovered. She is tracked to her coffin and killed with a wooden stake through her heart. Her body is then decapitated and burned.

While the sexual aspects of "Carmilla" are intriguing, the story is even more noteworthy for how it further popularized the vampire image. According to Le Fanu, a person becomes a vampire if he or she is bitten by one or commits suicide. While somewhat pale in appearance, and with two sharp, pointed teeth (that did not always show), Carmilla

A new twist was added to vampire literature in the late 1800s with the appearance of female vampires, depicted here in the 1992 film, Bram Stoker's Dracula.

otherwise was normal in appearance. She also was extremely strong and, while preferring the night, could operate during the day. Carmilla slept in a coffin, which she could enter and exit without leaving any trace, and she was also able to shape-shift into animal form, particularly that of a cat. Most of these traits would be picked up by other writers for use in their own vampire stories.

However, one piece of lore that Le Fanu introduced in "Carmilla" that was never adopted by other writers was the idea that a vampire could only choose a name that used the same combination of letters as his or her name in real life. Before she became a vampire, Carmilla had been the Countess Mircalla. After she rose from the dead, she also used the name Millarca.

"Carmilla," which appeared as one of a group of Le Fanu's stories in a volume called *In a Glass Darkly*, received widespread attention. Among those who read the story was a theater manager and part-time writer named Bram Stoker, who would soon create the ultimate vampire character.

Abraham Stoker was the author of Dracula, *a novel which has never been out of print since its publication in 1897.*

The Man Who Created Dracula

Abraham "Bram" Stoker was born on November 8, 1847, in Dublin, Ireland. For the first eight years of his life, he suffered from a debilitating leg ailment that prevented him from walking. Despite this handicap, when he finally did recover use of his legs, he grew quickly; and by age sixteen the red-haired Stoker was a hearty youth over six feet tall.

After graduating from Trinity College in Dublin in 1870, Stoker, like his father, became a civil service clerk at Ireland's seat of government, Dublin Castle. Possessed of a vivid imagination and a fondness for writing, Stoker found his job excruciatingly dull. Seeking relaxation at the theater, Stoker began working as an unpaid drama critic for the *Dublin Evening Mail* in November 1871. His favorable reviews of the performance of the English actor Sir Henry Irving gained Stoker the actor's friendship. In 1878 Irving asked Stoker to come to London to manage the Lyceum Theatre, which the actor had just purchased. Stoker immediately quit his civil service job and moved to London.

In his spare time, Stoker continued writing and produced numerous short stories and several novels over a decade. Then in April 1890 Stoker met Arminius Vambery, a Hungarian professor of Oriental languages at the University of Budapest, when Vambery was visiting London. Vambery told many stories about European legends and folklore, as well as factual accounts of such men as Prince Vlad Dracula of Romania.

Stoker had apparently been contemplating writing a vampire novel, brought on in part by a nightmare he had of a vampire rising out of its tomb. He also had read and enjoyed Le Fanu's short story "Carmilla." He let ideas of vampires simmer in his imagination for a time while he attended to the business of the Lyceum Theatre and did other writing. However, sometime later in 1890 he began work on the book that would come to be known as *Dracula*.

Dracula

Because of his many duties as theater manager, Stoker took several years to write *Dracula*, which was published in May 1897. The novel tells the story of Count Dracula, the king of the vampires. As portrayed by Stoker, Dracula is an old man dressed all in black, with white hair and a white mustache. He is very pale, with foul breath, pointed ears, a thick nose, sharp fingernails, and hair growing from the palms of his hands.

Stoker's plot revolved around Dracula's desire to leave his native Transylvania and go to London to prey upon the unsuspecting population. He retains a British real estate firm for this purpose and imprisons its agent Jonathan Harker in his castle when Harker visits him to finalize the purchase of a London estate. Once in London, Dracula attacks two women: the first, Lucy Westenra, turns into a vampire; the other is Mina Murray, the fiancée of Jonathan Harker. Fortunately, before Dracula can turn Murray into a vampire, he is thwarted by a group of men led by Abraham Van Helsing, a wise doctor who understands all about vampires. Unmasked, Dracula flees back to Transylvania but is pursued by Van Helsing and his group. In the end the vampire king is killed and crumbles to dust.

Despite the universal acclaim that the novel has today attained as an important work of fiction—it has never been out of print and has been the subject of more movie and stage adaptations than any novel in history—it was not an overwhelming success when it was first published. Some reviewers praised its diverse stable of characters and its creepy atmosphere, while others denounced it as strange and crude.

In Stoker's novel, the first woman Dracula attacks in London is Lucy Westenra, who becomes a vampire herself, as pictured here in the 1992 film, Bram Stoker's Dracula.

Stoker drew somewhat on established images of vampires to create his main character; in general appearance, Dracula is similar to Varney. However, the writer deliberately deviated from the image of the vampire as romantic villain or tragic hero that had become prevalent at the time. Stoker's Dracula is a coarse, almost animalistic creature that forces its will upon others. Due to his unattractive physical features, scenes in the book of women powerless to stop Dracula from drinking their blood are more like depictions of rape than romance.

Stoker's Dracula character was a combination of his own research into the supernatural and the differing images of vampires that were present in the Victorian era (aristocratic count, peasant returned from the dead, and so on). This image of a vampire, along with the powers Stoker gave Dracula, became the standard for all subsequent depictions of vampires. The author gave Dracula the ability to command the dead and animals as well—particularly small ones like rats, bats, owls, and foxes. The vampire could disappear at will and take on a variety of shapes, including that of a bat, a wolf, and a cloud of mist. His powers could be muted via the use of religious objects, garlic, and a wild rose. He could be destroyed by a stake though any part of his body, by shooting him while he lay in his coffin, and by decapitation. Dracula was also unable to cross running water except at high or low tide.

Financial Problems for Stoker

Unfortunately for Stoker, while *Dracula* was well received by the reading public, the novel did not earn him much money. The year after the book was published, things began going badly at the Lyceum, and the theater ultimately closed in 1902. By 1905 Stoker's only source of income was writing. He continued to scratch out a meager living via his pen, even as his health deteriorated. Stoker died on April 20, 1912, at age sixty-four.

One aspect of vampire legend, depicted here in a 1985 film, is the effectiveness of religious symbols like a cross as weapons against vampires.

But although *Dracula* did not bring either fame or fortune to Stoker during his lifetime, the novel did play an important role in the final transformation of the vampire image into the one that which is common today.

Popular Concepts

One popular concept of today's vampire that emerged from *Dracula* is the idea that the creature must rest in its native soil when it is not active. Stoker originated this idea, in part from the eastern European perception of vampires as reanimated corpses that rose from the local graveyard to terrorize the populace. Since that time the idea that a vampire requires its native soil has been used in many vampire stories and films.

It has become a tried-and-true tradition of vampire lore that religious symbols render the creature powerless. Images of a vampire cowering in fear before a crucifix or flinging his cape over his eyes and running away are common. Again, credit for this contribution to vampire lore must go to Stoker.

The contribution of Christianity to the vampire tradition brought new and powerful weapons to bear in the fight against Satan's minions, such as the cross, crucifix, holy water, and eucharistic wafer. As the image of vampires as reanimated corpses became typical, religious objects retained their value as an almost foolproof means of destroying the creatures or at least keeping them at bay.

Yet ironically, when vampires moved into popular culture and became fixtures of stories and novels, the religious aspect was largely ignored. Weapons used to fight the vampire were almost exclusively secular in nature, such as wooden stakes and garlic. If a priest appeared in any stories, it was usually as a minor character and not as the vampire's mortal foe. Stoker, however, reintroduced Christianity as an important force in vampire mythology. The use of religious items to fight Dracula abounds in the book, beginning in the very first chapter, when a rosary is presented as an object of protection to Harker. Since that time religious objects have played significant roles in vampire films, stories, and novels.

From the Heart to the Neck

Another piece of modern vampire tradition that can be traced directly to Stoker is having the creature bite its victims on the neck. Before *Dracula* vampires usually bit their victims over the heart. This was because, traditionally, the heart was where the emotions resided, so a bite there became all the more insidious because it was as if the creature were trying to suck out a person's soul. Stoker changed the bite location to the neck, possibly because this is where the jugular vein is located and a great quantity of blood can be obtained from this area very quickly.

Sunlight and Vampires

All of Stoker's copyrights passed to his wife, Florence, upon his death. She guarded them zealously, since she needed the money from the novel's royalties. Thus in 1921, when a German film company made a silent movie based on *Dracula* that they called *Nosferatu* (a word derived from ancient Greek, meaning "plague carrier") without first obtaining permission, Florence Stoker sued them. She won, and all copies of the film were ordered destroyed. However, some survived and the movie can be seen today. In fact, it is this film that some researchers point to as the origin for one of the most popular aspects of vampire lore: the creature's aversion to sunlight.

One of the most fondly held of all beliefs about vampires is that they cannot survive in sunlight. Scenes of vampires crumbling into dust or bursting into flame when exposed to the light of day are an integral part of vampire films and literature. However, the idea of sunlight as fatal to vampires is a modern invention. Early vampires could live and function during the day. Although many operated at night, it was not because they were forced to but because darkness was the best time for them to go about their nefarious business.

Similarly, early literary vampires were unaffected by sunlight. These creatures moved about during the day, although they preferred the cover of darkness. In Dracula's case, sunlight greatly reduced his power and made him easier to defeat. In one memorable scene in the novel, Dracula is attacked late in the afternoon and due to his weakened condition barely escapes by jumping out a window.

Many researchers point to *Nosferatu* as the first work in which a vampire is depicted being destroyed by sunlight. In the climactic final scene, the vampire Graf Orlock disappears in a puff of smoke when struck by dawn's first light. From there the idea spread to other vampire movies and stories.

The vampire in the 1921 German film, Nosferatu, *was destroyed by sunlight.*

However, there are others who feel that the effect of this film on vampire mythology has been exaggerated. As author of *The Vampire Book*, J. Gordon Melton, writes: "While *Nosferatu* emerged as an important film, it was for all practical purposes not available until the 1960s [due to a copyright dispute] and thus may have had less effect on the development of the vampire's image than many suspect."[14] It would be a play based on Stoker's book and a somewhat later film that would fix in modern minds the vampire's image.

Dracula Comes to the Stage

In the early 1920s, a playwright and director named Hamilton Deane bought the rights to *Dracula* from Florence Stoker in order to bring the novel to the stage. When he could not find a scriptwriter to adapt the book, Deane did it himself in a month, during a period when his other activities were limited due to a bad cold. And in casting the play, he took for himself the role of Van Helsing.

Deane made several changes in the plot for the sake of simplicity, including deleting the portions of the story that occur in Transylvania. He also made Dracula a member of European royalty so that he would fit easily into London's high society, which was the backdrop for Deane's revised story. Thus Deane dressed the vampire king in formal evening clothes and an opera cloak with a large stand-up collar. A simple cape had previously been standard attire for vampires. However, Deane needed the large collar of an opera cloak to hide the head of the actor who was playing Dracula, so that he could "disappear" through a trapdoor onstage

With Hamilton Deane's revisions for the stage depiction of his story, Dracula became more stylish and his trademark high-collared opera cloak appeared, as seen here in the 1979 movie, Dracula.

during a moment in the play. The actor would turn his back to the audience, and the high collar would hide his head. He then dropped through the trapdoor, leaving the cape to fall to the floor and making it seem as if he had vanished. Deane also refined Dracula's character, removing many of the rough edges and unattractive physical attributes that Stoker had given him so that his Dracula would be welcome among Britain's aristocracy.

Although he was unaware of it at the time, Deane had added significantly to the modern-day perception of a vampire. Once his play beccame a hit, his transformation of Dracula from a coarse and brutal creature to an elegantly dressed, refined nobleman became the standard by which all vampires were measured. Just one final piece of the puzzle remained to be put in place—this one by a Hungarian-born actor who barely knew English.

The Modern Vampire

Dracula was a huge success on stage. People came to see it so often that they memorized entire scenes and shouted out the lines before the actors could say them. Hoping to duplicate this success in the United States, in 1927 Broadway producer Howard Liveright bought the American dramatic rights from Florence Stoker and hired newspaperman John L. Balderston to rewrite Deane's play. Balderston streamlined the story even further, dropping several characters and combining a few others into one person. When it came time to cast the lead role, Liveright and director John D. Williams chose a dark-eyed, dark-haired Hungarian immigrant whose work they had seen in other Broadway plays. His name was Bela Lugosi.

Born in Lugos, Hungary, on October 20, 1882, Lugosi had been an actor in his native land before immigrating to the United States in 1920. He had appeared both on Broadway and in silent films when tapped to play the vampire king. His Hungarian accent, dark good looks, and

With his Hungarian accent and good looks, Bela Lugosi transformed Dracula into a suave and mysterious sex symbol in the hugely successful 1931 film, Dracula.

aristocratic demeanor made him seem born to play the role of Dracula. As he later said: "There was no male vampire type in existence. Someone suggested an actor of the Continental School who could play any type, and mentioned me. It was a complete change from the usual romantic characters I was playing, but it was a success."[15]

Lugosi had a difficult time understanding English, and thus learned many of his lines phonetically. However, his unique diction combined with his accent contributed an air of mystery and danger to the character of Dracula. The play opened on Broadway on October 5, 1927, and was an instant success. It ran for 241 performances, then reopened on the West Coast, with touring companies running in both the East and Midwest.

The play proved so successful that the struggling Hollywood film company Universal Studios bought the rights to it and turned it into a movie. Released in February 1931, the movie *Dracula* was also a huge hit, and its profits helped Universal survive. Ironically, despite his great success in the role on Broadway, Lugosi was not considered for the lead in the film until casting was nearly complete. Several other actors were pursued to play Dracula before Lugosi was, and if film great Lon Chaney had not died of cancer in August 1930, he almost certainly would have been given the part.

The Transformation Is Complete

With Lugosi's success as Dracula, both on stage and in film, the transformation of the vampire from a simply dressed peasant reeking of earth and decay to a nattily attired, handsome European count exuding sexual magnetism was complete.

Lugosi's performance as Dracula—foreign, mysterious, handsome, suave, and courteous, with just the slightest hint of menace behind hypnotic eyes—turned both him and, by association, vampires into sex symbols. When Lugosi, with his dark good looks, advanced on a female victim and drew his black cape majestically around them both before sinking his teeth into her neck, many in the audience viewed it not as an attack by an evil entity, but as a romantic liaison.

Lugosi was well aware of his—and Dracula's—sexual appeal. For example, in an interview he noted that more than 97 percent of his fan mail came from women.

Of course, the introduction of sexuality into the vampire legend was not new. However, almost all of the encounters between humans and vampires prior to those portrayed in the first *Dracula* film had been forced, signifying rape rather than romance. In the most suggestive sexual scene in Stoker's book, Dracula invades Mina's bedroom and forces her to drink his blood from a cut on his chest. During the episode, as Stoker writes, Dracula's eyes were inflamed with "devilish passion."[16] Later, when Dracula is driven off and Mina regains control of herself, she acts like a rape victim.

But in the metamorphosis of Dracula from the novel to the stage and then the movie screen, the vampire became less a rapist and more a desirable bedroom partner. In successive portrayals, Dracula and his ilk were still sexual predators, but the lure of desire outweighed the danger. Sex with a vampire was known to be a hideously bad choice—but extremely hard to resist.

This image of the sexually alluring vampire was further refined through succeeding films. It reached full flower in the late 1970s, when handsome actor Frank Langella portrayed the best-looking and most sexually appealing Dracula of all time in both a revival of the play and a remake of the film.

Despite the surface similarities, twentieth-century depictions of Dracula are far different from what Stoker intended. As one researcher writes in *The Complete Vampire Companion*, Stoker would have been "appalled"[17] at the suave, sexy image of his vampire king. For him, Dracula was never intended to be a romantic hero.

The Origins of Coffins

It was not just the persona of the vampire itself that was changed by the film version of *Dracula*. Another aspect of the modern vampire image that *Dracula* added to the creature's mythology was the association of coffins with vampires.

Even when the concept of a vampire was being developed in the popular imagination into that of a reanimated corpse, a coffin was still not the creature's customary home, simply because most people could not afford them. Until relatively recent times, the dead were usually wrapped in burial shrouds and laid to rest in shallow graves.

By the early eighteenth century, the use of coffins was far more prevalent, but that still did not guarantee them a place in vampire tradition. The early literary vampires did not rest in coffins. Even Stoker did not require a coffin for Dracula.

The image of a sexy vampire was even more firmly established in popular culture when actor Frank Langella portrayed Dracula on both stage and screen in the 1970s.

It seems that the linkage of coffins with vampires stems from Universal's *Dracula* movie. An early scene in that film shows Dracula and his fellow vampires eerily rising out of coffins. Because of the dramatic and spooky connotations that coffins provided, they quickly became part of vampire lore and loom large in depictions of life as a vampire today.

The Vampire Today

The modern vampire of books, films, and television takes on a variety of guises. He or she can be a hero, villain, or a combination of both. Male vampires, at least, can be ugly

The image of vampires rising from coffins was dramatically introduced in the 1931 film version of Dracula.

and repulsive or handsome and desirable. The vampire can be a tortured soul, bemoaning his or her existence, or can be motivated by pure evil without a shred of decency, killing merely to satisfy an insatiable blood lust. And in what may be the most ironic twist of all, vampires can be objects of humor, such as the vampire comedy film *Love at First Bite*, starring George Hamilton.

Today's vampires are also much freer in regard to how they live their life. Crosses, garlic, sunlight, stakes, coffins filled with earth—all of these things may or may not affect them, depending on the circumstances. Writers and film-makers take whatever elements of the vampire tradition that suit their purpose and disregard the rest.

Indeed, the modern vampire has come a long way from its early roots among ancient cultures as a hellish demon with no redeeming qualities. A massive mythology has grown up around vampires that far outstrips any other fictional being.

Chapter 4

Can Vampires Be Explained?

Today people know that vampires are creatures of myths and legends. But do these legends have any basis in fact? Have there ever been real-life vampires?

The Real Dracula

Although the Dracula character created by Bram Stoker is fictional, the fact that there actually was a person named Vlad Dracula sometimes causes people to think that there must be some basis of truth for the depiction of Dracula as a vampire.

The real Vlad Dracula was born in approximately 1431 in Schässburg, Transylvania, which is today located in north central Romania. His father's name was Vlad Dracul; in Romanian "Dracul" means either "devil" or "dragon." Thus "Vlad Dracula" means "son of Dracul," or "son of the devil (or dragon)."

The elder Vlad seized the throne of the kingdom of Walachia, an area that in contemporary Romania would be located south of the Transylvania Alps. At the time, this area of Europe was under constant threat from the Turks of the Ottoman Empire. Throughout his life Dracul shifted his allegiances back and forth between the Muslim Turks and the neighboring remnants of the Christian Holy Roman Empire. During one period when he was allied

The fifteenth-century ruler of Walachia, Vlad Dracula, also known as Vlad Tepes, was notorious for torturing and murdering thousands of his subjects.

with the Turks, Dracul left his son as a hostage with them, as a way of demonstrating his loyalty. Young Dracula remained a hostage for four years, all the while building up an enormous reservoir of hatred for his hosts.

In December 1447 Dracul's flexible alliances caught up with him, and he was killed in a campaign launched by Hungarian Christians to remove him from the throne of Walachia. Eventually Dracula succeeded his father and became the ruler of Walachia in 1456. Anyone who might have thought that Dracula's reign would be an improvement over his father's was soon proved wrong. By some accounts, approximately forty thousand people were put to death by Dracula—enemies, friends who had fallen under suspicion, and just ordinary citizens who offended him somehow. Dracula's favorite type of torture was impalement. He would have a thick wooden stake driven into a person's body in such a way that the victim remained alive. Then the stake would be set into the ground, leaving the victim suspended helplessly in the air. Dracula's propensity for this type of punishment earned him the nickname Tepes, or the Impaler. Today he is commonly referred to as Vlad Tepes, or Vlad the Impaler.

Unmatched Cruelty

In an age known for its cruelty and barbarism, the savageness of Vlad Tepes stood alone. No one was safe from his murderous wrath. When his mistress claimed she was pregnant, Vlad had her stomach split open to prove it. When visiting ambassadors to his court did not remove their turbans quickly enough, Vlad had the turbans nailed to their heads. When a magnificent feast he was giving was interrupted by a group of beggars, he had them burned alive on the spot. And when a visitor complained of the screams and stench coming from the dying and dead whom he had impaled, Vlad had him impaled as well—only higher up, so that the screams and stench would not bother him.

Over the course of Dracula's six-year reign as head of Walachia, he was responsible for more deaths than any ruler until modern times. Even his contemporaries, no strangers to the use of torture and murder, denounced him. Yet Dracula was unaffected by the opinion of others. A famous woodcut shows him eating dinner while surrounded by those he had impaled. He was particularly ruthless

In this sixteenth-century woodcut, Vlad Dracula dines, surrounded by his impaled victims.

against his hated foe the Turks, whom he repeatedly fought in an effort to keep them out of Europe. On one infamous occasion, he reportedly impaled twenty thousand Turkish captives and displayed them in a mile-long semicircle outside of Walachia's capital city of Tîrgovişte to discourage other enemy troops from invading.

At some point either late in 1461 or early in 1462, the Turks finally ousted Dracula from the Walachian throne. He fled to Hungary but was imprisoned there because of his heinous reputation. Incredibly, due to the ever-shifting alliances in the region, he once again assumed control of Walachia in the summer of 1476, but by this time everyone knew what was coming and wanted to avoid another reign of terror. Dracula was assassinated either at the end of December 1476 or in early January 1477. Despite his brutality, today Dracula is considered a national hero in Romania for his role in fighting the Turks and keeping their invading armies at bay.

Some researchers believe that Bram Stoker first heard about Vlad Tepes during the visit of Professor Vambery to London in April 1890. Others think that the author encountered Dracula in an 1820 book that he was using for researching his intended vampire novel entitled *Account of the Principalities of Wallachia and Moldavia.* Either way, once Stoker discovered the cruel warlord, he decided to base his title character on him and gave his name to the book's vampire king.

Stoker used the name Dracula to lend his novel a feel of authenticity and reality, but beyond that there is little resemblance between the cruel ruler and the fictional vampire. (Vlad's fondness for impaling his victims and the use of a stake to kill a vampire are completely coincidental.) In addition, despite his abhorrent behavior, the real-life Dracula displayed no vampire characteristics. Nevertheless, the fact that Vlad Tepes was so bloodthirsty and his name is shared by the most famous vampire of all time has helped to perpetuate the idea that such creatures do exist.

While Vlad Dracula was certainly a barbarous and indiscriminate killer, he cannot be considered a "real-life" vampire. However, throughout the course of history, there have been people whose actions and beliefs make them appear to be emulating the actions of vampires.

The Bloody Countess

One of the most notorious examples of a person exhibiting vampirelike traits is the case of Countess Elizabeth Báthory. Born to a prominent family (Stephen Báthory, her cousin, became king of Poland) in 1560, Báthory was raised on her family's estate in Transylvania.

The angelic face of Countess Elizabeth Báthory belies her bloodthirsty nature.

In May 1575 she married Count Ferenc Nadasdy, a Hungarian nobleman. Nadasdy was a soldier and away from home much of the time, which gave Elizabeth ample opportunity to manage the affairs at Castle Sarvar, the Nadasdy family estate. This she did—with unrelenting cruelty.

The girl took a sadistic delight in inflicting cruel and unusual punishments on her primarily female servants for the slightest infraction. Eventually she began torturing them for no reason other than to satisfy her desire to witness others in pain. Beatings and jamming pins into sensitive body parts such as underneath the fingernails were two of her favorite methods of torture. In the winter she also favored stripping her victims, taking them out into the snow, and pouring water over them until they froze.

According to legend, at one point during one of Elizabeth's torture sessions, the blood of one of her victims spilled onto her skin, and she was struck by how smooth and supple the area became. Obsessed by the desire to stay young and beautiful, Elizabeth supposedly began draining her victims of their blood and then used it as a "beauty cream," even to the point of bathing in it.

After her husband died in 1604, Elizabeth was left alone, and her murderous behavior reached new heights. She reportedly even had a special torture device built containing numerous daggers and other sharp objects. She would thrust young girls into the fiendish device and close the door, then watch delightedly as the blood flowed out into a catch basin.

Some researchers today dismiss the stories of Elizabeth's desire for blood as exaggerations that have been added to her life story to make it seem even more horrible. Others, however, accept as fact her obsession with blood as an anti-aging product. What is not in dispute is that the number of victims—most of them young serving girls—that she tortured and killed was in the hundreds. After word of her activities seeped out and became so persistent that authorities could no longer ignore them, she was arrested in December 1610 and brought to trial, despite the fact that she was a member of an important aristocratic family. There a diary introduced into evidence revealed the names, in Elizabeth's own handwriting, of 650 people tortured and murdered by her and her few trusted accomplices. While her helpers were executed, Elizabeth's royal connections helped her escape that fate. Instead she was sealed up in a small room at her castle without windows or doors; the only light and air came from a few small openings through which food was passed to her. She spent the last years of her life in solitary confinement, dying on August 21, 1614.

Other "Human" Vampires

Although Elizabeth Báthory had an apparent fondness for human blood, she was not a vampire in the traditional sense of being a reanimated corpse. Other people, much closer to modern times, have not only exhibited a desire for blood, but have gone so far as to emulate the actions of vampires.

One of the most recent examples of a person acting like a vampire was the case of George John Haigh of Great Britain. As a young man in the early part of the twentieth century, Haigh frequently dreamed that he was in a forest of crosses that changed into trees dripping with blood. In the dream Haigh felt extremely tired until a man standing by one of the trees offered him a bowl of the blood to drink, which energized him. Haigh decided that this recurring dream was a message telling him to drink blood to maintain his vigor.

Armed with this belief, Haigh built a special room in his home into which he lured unsuspecting victims. There he would kill them, drain their blood, drink it, and then dissolve the bodies in acid. When he was finally caught in 1949, the lurid details of his crimes caused him to be dubbed the Vampire of London. He was tried, convicted, and executed.

Serial murderer George John Haigh (on stairs, in suit), known popularly as the Vampire of London, arrives for his trial in April 1949.

Another so-called "modern vampire" was Fritz Haarmann, called the Vampire of Hanover, who lived in Germany from the late nineteenth century until his death in 1925. Haarmann befriended young men on the streets of Hanover and brought them to his home, where he engaged in sex with them and sometimes killed them. In 1919 he was arrested and sent to prison for seven months because homosexual behavior was illegal in Germany. At this point, though, he was not suspected of murder. Released late in 1919, Haarmann met a man named Hans Grans, who became his lover. At this point Haarmann's career as a vampire began. He and Grans would entice young men back to their home. There they were murdered, usually by Haarmann, who would bite them on the neck and throat, and then he would drink some of the blood. Haarmann, who was a butcher, also supposedly ground up the bodies of some of his victims and turned them into some of the meats and sausages that he sold to his customers.

Eventually Haarmann and Grans were caught. The grisly details of their crimes caused a sensation throughout Germany. While he was charged with killing twenty-four people, it was suspected that the real total was more than double that number. Haarmann was executed in April 1925, while Grans was imprisoned for life.

"Real Vampires"—or Imagination?

Haigh and Haarmann are two of the best-known examples of what some would consider "real-life" vampires. However, there have been many other examples of serial killers who acted like vampires. Peter Kürten, dubbed the Monster of Duesseldorf and the Duesseldorf Vampire by the press, murdered over a dozen people from 1929 to 1930 and supposedly obtained sexual satisfaction from drinking their blood. In Paris in the late 1840s Francois Bertrand was called the Vampire for violating numerous graves, unearthing corpses, and then biting and mutilating them.

These are just a few of the many supposed instances of "real" vampirism that have occurred in more recent times.

Like Haigh and Haarmann, the people who performed these acts were not actually vampires but, rather, disturbed individuals for whom vampirelike behavior merely provided a convenient outlet for their strange compulsions. However, occasionally an incident of apparent vampirism has occurred that cannot be simply dismissed as the actions of a deranged person. One of the most striking of these is the strange story of the Highgate Vampire.

From the late 1960s through the early 1980s, reports of very unusual events emerged from the Cemetery of St. James in the Highgate section of London. (Ironically, this was the same cemetery used by Bram Stoker in *Dracula* as the burial place of Lucy Westenra, a victim of the vampire's attacks.)

Beginning in 1967 a ghostly figure was repeatedly seen in the cemetery at night. At the same time a schoolgirl named Elizabeth Wojdyla and her friend told Sean Manchester, head of the Vampire Research Society, that they had seen the dead coming out of their graves in Highgate. Wojdyla also reported that she had experienced nightmares in which an evil entity tried to enter her bedroom.

After apparently subsiding for a while, Wojdyla's nightmares returned in 1969, and now the malevolent entity actually entered her bedroom. Soon she began exhibiting symptoms of pernicious anemia—the classic medical diagnosis

Unusual events occurring at London's Cemetery of St. James from the late 1960s through the 1980s kept belief in vampires alive among some people.

cited in films and stories whenever a vampire has been preying upon a victim. In addition, Wojdyla had two small wounds on her neck. When the girl's room was filled with garlic and crosses and holy water was placed in it, her condition improved.

More Sightings

Meanwhile, sightings of supernatural entities continued at Highgate. The bodies of animals, some drained of their blood, were found in the cemetery and a nearby park. Then another woman began having the same symptoms as Wojdyla. While sleepwalking, she led Manchester to a group of aboveground crypts in Highgate. In March 1970 Manchester and two others entered one of these crypts and found three empty coffins. They lined the coffins with garlic and placed a cross in each; both of these were traditional safeguards against vampires. On a subsequent trip into another Highgate vault, Manchester found what he believed to be an actual vampire. Reading an exorcism, he sealed the vault with cement mixed with garlic.

Things quieted down for a time, but then in 1977 Manchester began investigating a mansion near Highgate Cemetery that was rumored to be haunted. Upon investigation, a casket was found in the home's basement and brought outside. When Manchester opened the casket, he saw inside what he believed was the same vampire that he had seen several years earlier in Highgate. This time he staked the body, which he reported turned into a slimy, foul-smelling mass. He then burned the coffin.

While some might have expected this to be the end of the Highgate Vampire, such was not the case. In 1980 reports of dead animals drained of blood again being found in the area caused concern. Manchester thought it to be the work of someone who had been turned into a vampire by the Highgate Vampire he claimed to have killed. He traced the entity to Great Northern London Cemetery. There, one evening in 1982, he encountered a creature resembling a spider but as large as a cat. He staked the creature. When dawn approached, the creature reportedly turned back into human form. Manchester buried these remains, and no reports of similar incidents have since emerged from Highgate.

Was this a true case of vampirism, a hoax, or merely a series of natural occurrences in which people let their imaginations run wild? No one knows for certain, but it is reports of incidents like that of the Highgate Vampire that keep belief in vampires alive.

Catalepsy as an Explanation for Vampirism

While serial murders and hoaxes undoubtedly account for some supposed incidences of vampirism, there are other

Modern reports of vampire activity are sometimes based on the activities of serial killers. Here pathologists examine evidence in such a case.

possible explanations for what was once considered evidence of a vampire's presence. For example, a medical condition known as catalepsy might well have caused people in ages past to believe in vampires.

The victim of a cataleptic attack is temporarily in a state of suspended animation that mimics death. The muscles become rigid, and all vital signs, such as breathing and heart rate, slow to the point of being almost nonexistent. The victim sees and hears everything going on around him or her but cannot respond. Even trained physicians have been fooled into thinking that a person suffering from catalepsy has died. Thus it is not surprising that in earlier centuries, when people with little or no medical training were caring for the sick, someone who had suffered a cataleptic attack would have been mistakenly pronounced dead.

Terror for Some Cataleptics

For the victim of catalepsy, being pronounced dead was only the beginning of the horror. Before embalming became common in Europe, it was entirely possible that a victim of catalepsy would revive after having been buried. It can only be imagined how frantically people buried alive would have struggled for freedom: clawing at the earth, tearing away fingernails and flesh, even frantically chewing their burial shroud, before finally suffocating. Thus when those searching for a suspected vampire opened the grave and found the corpse in such a disheveled state, they naturally would have assumed that its condition was the result of its having left its grave and roamed about.

Even in the absence of catalepsy, premature burial was a distinct possibility in ages past. Particularly during times of plague, there was great haste to get bodies into the ground. People were so afraid of contracting plague themselves that as soon as sick people stopped moving, they were considered dead and removed from the home as quickly as possi-

ble. Burial almost always occurred within twenty-four hours after death.

This expediency, however, did not help someone who had, for example, lapsed into a coma. The noted twentieth-century English folklorist Montague Summers, who believed in the existence of vampires, felt that premature burial "may have helped to reinforce the tradition of the vampire and the phenomenon of vampirism."[18]

During the Black Death, people terrified of contracting the plague buried the dead so quickly that some were buried alive. Victims of such a fate who were later exhumed could have been mistakenly identified as vampires.

Porphyria

Other medical conditions also may account for a few reports of vampire activity. In the mid-1980s a series of metabolic disorders known collectively as porphyria were said by some medical authorities to be a possible cause of vampirelike behavior. A victim of porphyria is unable to properly synthesize heme, which is part of hemoglobin, the oxygen-carrying

According to one discredited theory, a medical condition known as porphyria could have led to both a craving for blood and an aversion to sunlight.

component of red blood. In addition to anemia, an extreme case of porphyria causes great sensitivity to light.

Some researchers speculated that in centuries past, before porphyria was treatable with injections of heme, a person suffering from the condition might feel compelled to drink blood in order to satisfy a craving for heme. This, combined with an aversion to sunlight, could have explained some cases of vampirism, according to the theory.

The possibility that there could have been a medical explanation for vampirism—and, therefore, real-life vampires—created a sensation in the modern media. Radio, television, and newspapers all gave the story extensive coverage, often with humorous headlines, such as the one that appeared in *Newsweek*: "Vampire Diagnosis: Real Sick."[19]

Critics of the theory quickly charged that any link between porphyria and vampirism made little sense, since there was no evidence that sufferers would have gained any relief from their symptoms by drinking blood. Even more distressed were the tens of thousands of people suffering from porphyria who suddenly found themselves the butt of jokes about vampires. As Norine Dresser writes in *American Vampires: Fans, Victims, Practitioners:*

> To have porphyria is no laughing matter. Yet porphyria patients immediately became the targets of jokes and victims of avoidance, fear, and derision as a result of the publicity blitz ignited by the hypothesis. The association of the relatively unknown porphyria with the very well known vampire set off a chain reaction of unexpected and unpleasant events because the allure of the vampire is so strong in this country [America].[20]

Today porphyria as an explanation of vampirism has been completely discredited. But just the fact that modern medical practitioners would debate such a possibility indicates how deeply ingrained vampires are in the human imagination.

Other Explanations

Other evidence for the existence of vampires, such as the lack of decay in certain corpses, can also be explained by modern science. The nature of the illness that killed a person, the temperature of the ground where the body was buried, and the presence and/or lack of certain elements in the earth could all have retarded decomposition of a body, leading superstitious villagers to conclude that the corpse was inhabited by a vampire. Moreover, only in relatively recent times were the dead buried in tightly sealed coffins, in which anaerobic bacteria cause the quickest and most extreme decay.

Finally, tradition in some cultures held that a vampire would gnaw at its own body parts first, before rising from the grave and heading out to menace living humans. Since the dead were buried hastily in shallow graves, animals often preyed upon the bodies. Thus when the suspected vampire was exhumed, "evidence" was there for the superstitious to see.

Belief Is a Powerful Thing

In general, it is likely that many different factors contributed to the overall belief in vampires. As with other legends, those who believe in them readily accept even the flimsiest evidence to sustain those beliefs. As author J. Gordon Melton writes in *The Vampire Book:*

> A consideration of the strengths and limitations of many explanations of vampires suggest that the belief in vampirism is a very old and possibly cultural response to an event that happens in all cultures— the untimely death of a loved one as a result of childbirth, accident, or suicide, followed by an intense experience of interacting with the recently dead person. Given that belief, there are a variety of events, such as the irregular rate of decay of the soft flesh of corpses, that could be cited as visible "proof" that vampires exist or as factors that on occasion correlate to their presence. Since "unnatural" deaths still occur, and people still have intense experiences with the dead . . . those people who also believe in vampires can point to those experiences as in some manner substantiating their belief. Thus, these experiences indicate the presence of vampires. . . . [W]e know vampires exist because of these experiences.[21]

The State of Vampirism Today

While it is impossible to determine how extensive an actual belief in vampires is today throughout the world, it is far easier to see that interest in vampires has never been greater. Vampires are seemingly everywhere, from cereal boxes to movie screens, and it appears unlikely that they will be retreating into their coffins anytime soon.

Vampire images are prevalent in the popular media today, as reflected in the 1994 film Interview with the Vampire, *starring Brad Pitt (pictured here).*

In the United States alone, numerous vampire societies and fan clubs have sprung up, dedicated to studying and celebrating everything vampiric. The names of these groups range from the Count Dracula Fan Club to the Vampire Research Center. Members of such organizations are primarily interested in the long history and tradition of vampires.

Vampires have also been featured performers in popular entertainment. Every few years seem to bring a new cycle of films starring the legendary bloodsuckers. However, while some movies opt for the traditional vampire in formal wear with a mysterious foreign accent, others seek to reinvent the image. Thus vampires have appeared as heroes, detectives, next-door neighbors, rowdy teenagers, and in a variety of other guises far removed from the stereotypical suave foreigner in evening clothes.

Television has also helped keep vampires popular. Just as in films, the undead have played a variety of roles on TV; some portraits are more traditional in nature—villains attacking people and drinking their blood—while others have broken the mold and featured vampires as heroes and sympathetic characters. For a time in the 1960s, a vampire was even the star of a TV soap opera called *Dark Shadows*. The show was saved from cancellation thanks to the popularity of Barnabas Collins, its vampire character. *Dark Shadows* went on to become a successful show and a profitable vampire franchise, spawning games, books, trading cards, and other memorabilia.

Popular literature has also helped propel the vampire to new heights. In recent years authors have been able to create elaborate new situations for the vampire to exist in—situations in which some, but not all, of the old guidelines still apply. Thus there are vampires that use sunblock to repel sunlight and so are able to survive during the day, vampires that walk on special shoes that contain soil from their native land so that they don't have to constantly lug coffins around, and vampires that can be shot, stabbed, and even staked but still survive. Like their creative counterparts in the movies and television, writers borrow whichever parts of traditional vampire mythology suit their purpose and discard the rest. The flexibility of the vampire tradition—as compared to that for other mythical creatures, whose existence is governed by more rigid standards—has helped to keep vampires popular subjects in the entertainment world.

Indeed, the modern image of vampires has changed so much that these once frightening creatures now even appeal to children. A popular breakfast cereal, Count Chocula, uses a cartoon vampire as its advertising symbol, while the children's television show *Sesame Street* has a vampire character simply named Count von Count, who helps toddlers learn about numbers.

A Continuing Fascination

Besides sheer entertainment value, what has kept alive humankind's fascination with vampires throughout the centuries? Even today, in a society dominated by science and technology, the legend of a creature that has existed since recorded history remains active and vibrant, and shows no signs of fading away.

One reason for the continuing popularity of vampires might be the lure of eternal life that the creature offers. Since the dawn of humanity, people have tried to figure out a way to cheat death, just as the vampire has done. The promise of immortality and eternal youth that the vampire represents is a powerful attraction for those who fear the aging process and death.

Others feel that continued fascination with vampires stems from the sexual aspects of the myth. The vampire sends out a variety of sexual signals: forced sex, intimacy with a mysterious and irresistible stranger, secret liaisons at night, and a visitor invading the bedroom without warning. As J. Gordon Melton writes in *The Vampire Book:* "From the beginning, a seductive sexuality has existed as an element of the . . . vampire commingling with that of the

Despite their evil reputation, vampires have even come to be seen as friendly creatures, like Count von Count on Sesame Street.

Simmering sexuality, the idea of eternal life, and pure entertainment value keep the vampire legend alive.

monstrous, and goes far to explain the vampire's appeal relative to its monstrous cousins."[22]

Still others are drawn to the nonconformist image of the vampire. A vampire is the ultimate outsider, living outside the laws of both God and humans and having no regard for either.

In the final analysis, it is likely that the vampire's continuing popularity stems in part from myriad factors. One thing seems certain, however: Having existed for thousands of years, and currently more popular than ever, the legend of the vampire does not seem in danger of crumbling into dust anytime soon.

Notes

Chapter One: The Vampire Experience

1. Olga Hoyt, *Lust for Blood*. Briarcliff Manor, NY: Stein and Day, 1984, p. 94.
2. Hoyt, *Lust for Blood*, p. 45.

Chapter Two: A Creature from the Mists of Time

3. Quoted in Hoyt, *Lust for Blood*, p. 33.
4. Quoted in Hoyt, *Lust for Blood*, p. 57.
5. Quoted in J. Gordon Melton, *The Vampire Book*. Detroit: Visible Ink Press, 1999, p. 777.
6. Quoted in Hoyt, *Lust for Blood*, p. 92.
7. Quoted in Hoyt, *Lust for Blood*, p. 106.
8. Quoted in Hoyt, *Lust for Blood*, p. 103.
9. Quoted in Rosemary Ellen Guiley, *The Complete Vampire Companion*. New York: Macmillan, 1994, p. 16.
10. Quoted in Hoyt, *Lust for Blood*, p. 104.
11. Quoted in Melton, *The Vampire Book*, p. 87.

Chapter Three: Vampires in Popular Culture

12. Melton, *The Vampire Book*, p. 589.

13. Quoted in Hoyt, *Lust for Blood*, p. 139.
14. Melton, *The Vampire Book*, p. 661.
15. Quoted in Arthur Lennig, *The Count*. New York: G. P. Putnam's Sons, 1974, p. 66.
16. Quoted in Melton, *The Vampire Book*, p. 615.
17. Quoted in Guiley, *The Complete Vampire Companion*, p. 68.

Chapter Four: Can Vampires Be Explained?

18. Quoted in Melton, *The Vampire Book*, p. 242.
19. Quoted in Norine Dresser, *American Vampires: Fans, Victims, Practitioners*. New York: W. W. Norton, 1989, p. 174.
20. Dresser, *American Vampires*, p. 179.
21. Melton, *The Vampire Book*, p. 243.
22. Melton, *The Vampire Book*, p. 620.

For Further Reading

Thomas G. Alyesworth, *The Story of Vampires*. New York: McGraw-Hill, 1977. A volume of vampire stories from around the world.

——, *Vampires and Other Ghosts*. Reading, MA: Addison-Wesley, 1972. A book that discusses vampires, ghosts, and other supernatural creatures.

Elwood D. Baumann, *Vampires*. New York: Franklin Watts, 1977. An examination of the facts and legends that surround vampires.

Daniel C. Scavone, *Vampires*. San Diego: Greenhaven Press, 1990. A book that looks at both sides of the question as to whether vampires exist.

David J. Skal, *V Is for Vampire: The A–Z Guide to Everything Undead*. New York: Plume, 1996. An alphabetical listing of many topics associated with vampires.

Works Consulted

Paul Barber, *Vampires, Burial, and Death*. New Haven, CT: Yale University Press, 1988. A comprehensive look at burial customs throughout the world and how they relate to the myth of vampires.

Basil Copper, *The Vampire in Legend and Fact*. Secaucus, NJ: Citadel Press, 1974. The story of vampires in both folklore and popular culture.

Norine Dresser, *American Vampires: Fans, Victims, Practitioners*. New York: W. W. Norton, 1989. An examination of vampires in the United States.

Rosemary Ellen Guiley, *The Complete Vampire Companion*. New York: Macmillan, 1994. A book that combines vampire legends and lore with interviews with writers and directors of vampire novels and films.

Olga Hoyt, *Lust for Blood*. Briarcliff Manor, NY: Stein and Day, 1984. A volume that traces vampire legends and lore throughout the centuries.

Arthur Lennig, *The Count*. New York: G. P. Putnam's Sons, 1974. A biography of Bela Lugosi.

Raymond T. McNally, *A Clutch of Vampires*. New York: Warner, 1974. A book of vampire fact and fiction by one of the pioneers of vampire research.

J. Gordon Melton, *The Vampire Book*. Detroit: Visible Ink Press, 1999. An extremely extensive alphabetical listing of everything concerning vampires.

Index

Picture Credits

About the Author

Russell Roberts graduated from Rider University in Lawrenceville, New Jersey. A full-time freelance writer, he has published over 250 articles and short stories, and eleven nonfiction books: *Stolen: A History of Base Stealing, Down the Jersey Shore, Discover the Hidden New Jersey, All About Blue Crabs and How to Catch Them, 101 Best Businesses to Start, Ten Days to a Sharper Memory, Endangered Species, Ancient Egyptian Rulers, Lincoln and the Abolition of Slavery, Presidential Scandals*, and *Vietnam Generals and Politicians*.

He currently resides in Bordentown, New Jersey, with his family and a cat named Rusti that is far too lazy to even jump over a corpse.